THE SCHOOL OF ART

WRITTEN BY TEAL TRIGGS
ILLUSTRATED BY DANIEL FROST

WIDE EYED EDITIONS

Welcome to the School of Art

STUDENT'S NAME

Contents

Term 1

Term 2

What design principles help us to make art?

Term 3

What can you do with your newfound skills?

LETTER OF ACCEPTANCE
TO THE
SCHOOL OF ART

CONGRATULATIONS,

_____

PLEASE JOIN US ON THE
FIRST DAY OF TERM.
BEST WISHES,

Professors of the School of Art

School of Art

Dear Student,

So, you want to make great art? As a creative person, your journey begins here, at the School of Art.

We are your five professors. Each of us is good at different things—like making things, having ideas, and using our senses—and we are here to guide you through 40 lessons that explore new and different ways to make your own creative works.

Try out the activities on every page, and work with us to understand how flat shapes become three-dimensional, to learn fun ways of creating patterns, to explore why color makes us feel happy or sad… and lots more! As you enter the School of Art, remember you are here to learn but by all means do have fun! Study hard, and creative success will be yours.

We look forward to seeing you on the first day of the new term!

the Professors

What is an art school?

Hello new students! We are very happy that you have joined us here to be introduced to some of the basic ideas behind the great works of art.

This book has been put together by your five professors, who have had enormous fun working on 40 lessons for you to try out. We like to think that each of us may bring something new and unique to your education in art and design. Each lesson will be conducted in one of our five studios—we like to think we have the most creative classrooms in the world! We will introduce and help explain the basic elements and principles of art and design. There is even a section on how to apply what you learn from these lessons to the world outside the School of Art. We like to think that art and design can help change how we look at the world.

You will have a chance to meet each of us in our studios and to practice what you have learned through a range of activities at the end of each lesson. As a student, you will also be asked to display some of your final art and design work at the annual School of Art exhibition! This work could take the form of a painting, a sculpture, or a poster and can be made using traditional methods such as paintbrushes, crayons, or collage, or could even be made digitally on your computer. People come from all over the world to see what students have made during their time at the School of Art. What we hope that you will bring to our school is your creative imagination and enthusiasm to learn about how art and design can make a difference to each of us in our daily lives.

But what does attending an art school actually mean?

You might think that the School of Art looks like any other school. But you will soon find out that lessons here are quite different than any you have experienced before. This is a place full of creative energy, and our imaginative students come from around the world to make things together. We like to experiment and take risks—doing things we haven't done before—and look forward to having you join us!

Here, art can take many forms, from ceramics to jewelry, sculpture, and painting, as well as graphic design, sound design, animation, illustration, fashion, textile design, and product design, where we think about the design things we use every day, from toothbrushes to televisions! And, while we like to make new things here, we also teach students about the history of art and design.

We think drawing is very important, as it teaches you how to see, and suggest you keep a sketchbook. This will help you to show us your ideas, work out solutions to problems, and answer the challenges you might face along the way. The 40 lessons in this book will introduce you to basic design principles. Each lesson is followed by an activity or a brief, where you are asked to try out what you have learned during the lesson. There are no right or wrong answers! Use the activities as a chance to do something you haven't done before and experiment with new ideas about what you have just learned.

We hope that your time at the School of Art will help you think differently about and look at the world around you in new and exciting ways. You are about to embark on an amazing learning journey.

Now it's time to come and meet each of us in our studios.

FOLLOW ME AND LET'S GET STARTED!

Why are ideas important in art and design?

HELLO!

I'd like to introduce myself. I am the Professor of Ideas and have had many enjoyable years teaching students, like you, in the School of Art.

WHY ARE IDEAS IMPORTANT IN ART AND DESIGN?

An idea is an intangible thing—something that is hard to hold on to. Ideas are thoughts that live in your head. In order to make an idea tangible, you need to give it form. I think ideas are important when you are making art because they can make you look at the world differently in order to create new things.

WHAT IS MY JOB AT THE SCHOOL OF ART?

As Professor of Ideas, I have an important role to play in the School of Art. The small, pink, billowy cloud that is always hovering above my head is full of exciting ideas. I like to come up with thoughts, plans, or suggestions about what the other professors and students might want to make and do in the School of Art. I love to collaborate—an important word here, which means working with other people. So, when you need an idea, please just pluck one out of my cloud!

SO WHAT DO I GET UP TO HERE?

Like a swan on water, I glide through the school's corridors and studios in order to help provide inspiration to our students, spurring them on to make their best work. I love clothes, which are a very creative way to express yourself, and my prize possessions are my several long strands of white pearls. My pearls help me explain the ideas that inform our lessons. Of course, I also have a very smart cat who sometimes assists me. Her name is Fluffy. Oh, and sometimes I like to be mischievous and play practical jokes on the other professors—for purely professional reasons, of course!

WHAT WILL YOU FIND INSIDE MY STUDIO?

My studio is very simple: a pale blue space with no walls. But within this space floats a roomful of white clouds. Each cloud holds hundreds of new ideas. It is a studio of possibilities. There are no boundaries for my imagination, and nor should there be for yours.

In the School of Art we want to create experiences and ensure our ideas are relevant to future societies. Together, the professors and students have the ability to make wonderful new worlds for people to live and play in happily.

Why are form and shape important in art and design?

NICE TO MEET YOU

I am the Professor of Form. I might seem a bit shy, and sometimes a bit fussy! But don't let that stop you from saying hello—behind my wire-rimmed glasses and pointy beard, I am a friendly chap!

WHY ARE FORM AND SHAPE IMPORTANT IN ART AND DESIGN?

Ideas are all well and good, but as artists and designers we need to make those ideas come to life. In order to do this, we create shapes—which are flat, or two-dimensional—and, forms, which are three-dimensional, with height, width, and depth.

WHAT IS MY JOB AT THE SCHOOL OF ART?

My role at the School of Art is to help the Professor of Ideas and the students develop their ideas, turning them into visible, tangible, touchable things. That's even true when they are created inside a computer, which is a "virtual" space and which you will learn more about when you meet the Professor of Making.

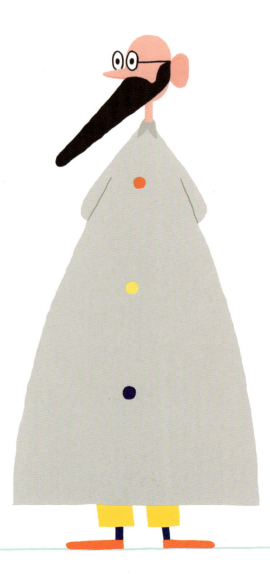

SO WHAT DO I GET UP TO HERE?

Many, many years ago (1919–1933 to be exact), there was another famous art school called the Bauhaus, in Germany. One of the Bauhaus "masters" was a man named Johannes Itten, whom I greatly admired—and not just because he also had a bald head and wore wire-rimmed glasses like me!

Johannes Itten taught composition and color to students, and like him, I teach the fundamentals of basic design at our School of Art. I was inspired by Itten to design my own uniform for the School of Art, which I am wearing now.

WHAT WILL YOU FIND INSIDE MY STUDIO?

My studio in the school is organized on a nine-square grid, with the fundamental points, lines, planes, and volumes hanging neatly from my ceiling. On a nearby shelf I keep my "visual grammar," a kind of language for the School of Art, which is based upon the basic shapes: circles, squares, and triangles. We use these in order to give form and shape to the thoughts of the Professor of Ideas and, of course, all our students!

How do art and design make us use our senses?

GOOD DAY, NEW STUDENT!

I am the Professor of Senses. I haven't lost my curiosity, even though I am now quite an old man! I like to ask lots of questions of our professors and students in the School of Art.

HOW DO ART AND DESIGN MAKE US USE OUR SENSES?

I like to think that you don't just *see* art, you *experience* it. Of course sight is very important, but my favorite kinds of art activate your other senses, too; things that use sound, smell, touch, or even taste can be more exciting and memorable than something that is just for looking at!

WHAT IS MY JOB AT THE SCHOOL OF ART?

My role at the School of Art is to develop projects that use the five senses. Depending on the experience I have when I encounter an artwork, my physical features can grow in response! For example, if the project deals with sound, my ears grow bigger; if it has to do with touch, my fingers grow longer. Using my senses, I help to create interesting experiences for others, too.

SO WHAT DO I GET UP TO HERE?

Out of all the professors, I have been at the School of Art the longest. I was even a student here in my younger days, but that was quite some time ago, as you can probably tell! I like to look smart for our lessons and always wear one of my striped knitted ties and best blue socks. My guilty pleasure in life? I love ice cream! Especially if it is served in a pointy sugar cone.

WHAT WILL YOU FIND INSIDE MY STUDIO?

My studio is the brightest, loudest, and nicest-smelling studio in the School of Art. It is full of big, wacky-looking machines that are for measuring and understanding our senses. All the professors and students come here to experiment and use our imaginations. We take our jobs very seriously, but sometimes the best art comes from being playful!

What different things can we use to make art?

HOWDY!

I am the Professor of Making. I love to make things: big as well as small things; physical things and also digital things.

WHAT DIFFERENT THINGS CAN WE USE TO MAKE ART?

Certain things might come to mind when you think about art—crayons, paints, paper, and so on—and you are right, you can use these to make art, but I am here to show you that really, you can make art from anything. That's right—ANYTHING! One famous artist, called Marcel Duchamp, even used a urinal once! So together, we will learn how to create different kinds of art using different materials.

WHAT IS MY JOB AT THE SCHOOL OF ART?

I am responsible for the different laboratories as well as the technical workshops where you can find the materials out of which shape and form are created. I often work with the Professor of Form and transform his sketches into objects using materials such as paper, glass, stone, wood, metal, ceramics, and woven textiles.

SO WHAT DO I GET UP TO HERE?

I am very proud of our new digital and rapid-prototyping labs, where we are exploring new ways of making things. It's a very exciting time for digital technologies. However, we never forget to experiment with older, more traditional ways of making things, too. This is what makes studying at the School of Art so varied and interesting.

One thing I'd like to note: we are very concerned for your safety in our workshops. I will always ask you to check with an adult before using any sharp tools or glues. I want you to have fun with making, but always remember: safety first!

WHAT WILL YOU FIND INSIDE MY STUDIO?

I've recently discovered 3-D digital printing and my studio has become a wonderland of three-dimensional printed objects.

A few days ago, I tried to create a new pair of shoes to go with my overalls. My shoe experiment went very well. Okay, except that I put the wrong size into the computer! The shoes were so big they wouldn't fit into my studio locker, so I had to start all over again.

Now I am making my second pair of shoes—and they are even better! What the heck, a girl can never have too many shoes.

How can art and design make people's lives better?

GREETINGS!

It is with great pleasure that I introduce myself to you. I am the Professor of the Planet. I am the newest professor in the School of Art.

WHAT MADE ME WANT TO MAKE ART?

Before I joined the School of Art, I used to travel all over the world. I worked on interesting projects with local communities to help find solutions to the challenges they faced. We made things together. I learned a lot about other cultures and their hopes for the planet and I came to believe that art can play a role in improving the world around us.

WHAT IS MY JOB AT THE SCHOOL OF ART?

The other professors say that I am the school's moral compass—I help us to think about the world around us a bit more in everything we do. The planet is a wonderful place with lots of wildlife, oceans, and amazing landscapes, and I try to make us more aware of the issues around sustainability, climate change, and the environment.

HOW CAN ART AND DESIGN MAKE PEOPLE'S LIVES BETTER?

I champion ways in which art and design can improve people's lives and protect our planet for future generations. As students here, you don't have to think about solving *all* the big challenges of the world. That is too much for anybody! But, you can explore new ways of making small changes at home or with other students. If everyone in the School managed to solve one small problem, then collectively we would make a huge difference!

WHAT WILL YOU FIND INSIDE MY STUDIO?

My studio is a greenhouse at the very top of the School of Art, filled with unusual tropical plants. I love to grow bromeliads, which come from the Amazon rain forest. Their leaves form bowl shapes that collect rainwater naturally.

As you have seen, all the professors have individual characteristics that make us a bit different from other people. Mine is that I have learned how to float above the ground. This can be good fun—and useful, too!

The School of Art is a place where you can be who you want to be. Don't be afraid to let your individuality shine through!

What basic elements do we need to make art?

In this first term, we will be learning about the basic elements of art. But what are they, and why do we need them?

Imagine what it would be like if there weren't any lines, shapes, or textures in the world. What would it be like if we saw everything in black and white? If we couldn't experience depth and space, our world would be two-dimensional and flat.

Design is all around us in our everyday lives. If you look outside your window, what do you see? Perhaps, if you live in a city, you might see cars and buses driving down the road. Across the street you may see tall skyscraper buildings, where office workers are sitting behind computers. Nearly everything in a city has been designed to make it a better place for the people who live there. A designer's job is to determine what things look like, as well as making sure they meet our needs.

If you live in the countryside, you can see nature's own designed environment. For example, the rings that you can count on the trunk when a tree is cut down tell you its age; the butterfly that perches effortlessly on a flower has a pattern on its wings that helps it blend into the background, and the snail has a shell on its back that it uses for protection. Nature is also an ecosystem where living and nonliving elements work together. For example, soil, water, and light help plants grow.

It is useful to understand which basic elements make up our natural and person-made environments. The basic elements are what artists use to make a piece of work: line, shape, geometric form, space, color, pattern, and texture. By designing or arranging these elements, we can communicate ideas and choose something's structure or function. This design might even change how people behave—like with the markings on soccer fields or roads.

In our first lessons at the School of Art, we will introduce you to basic design elements and explore how they work. The Professor of Ideas will help us discover how a line begins and what kinds of lines we can make with a ball of string. Lines can also make shapes. The Professor of Form shows us how flat shapes can magically change from two-dimensional flat objects, such as squares, into things that fill a three-dimensional space, like cubes.

In the Professor of the Planet's Greenhouse Studio, we will learn about shadows, texture, shading, and pattern—and where to find these in nature. See if you can glimpse the Professor of Form peering out of the bushes with a spotted butterfly on his head!

The basic elements come alive when the Professor of the Senses discusses how we show direction. Join the professors as they experiment with movement—and don't fall over!

The final lessons of the term look in detail at an important basic design element: color. Make a giant color wheel with the Professor of Making and get out your painting smocks and paintbrushes as we mix colors to look lighter, darker, and brighter. Explore complementary colors, which are on opposite sides of the color wheel, and experiment with a trick of the eye that explains what happens when you look at a color for too long! And finally, how do colors affect our moods? The Professor of Senses explains how different color combinations can cause different reactions. Today he is wearing yellow and is very happy to be working with you.

So, turn the page and let's begin!

How does a line begin?

It was the first day of term! The professors were gathered together, ready for their first lesson.

"Let's get to the point, shall we?" said the Professor of Ideas, adding, "What is a point?" The Professor of Form reached up and took down from a hook on the studio's ceiling a small circle.

"A point on its own looks like this: a small dot. If you put a pen to paper, you will create a dot, which we also call a point."

"However," chimed in the Professor of Making, "if you keep your pen on the paper and allow it to move—in any direction— your point will become a line."

"That's right!" said the Professor of Ideas, continuing, "Lines are made up of a number of points that are sitting close together."

ACTIVITY

Take a felt-tip pen. Can you create a line by drawing lots of dots next to one another, like pearls on a necklace? Next, draw two dots. Join them, first with a straight line, and then with a curved one.

LINES ARE MADE UP OF A NUMBER OF POINTS SITTING NEXT TO EACH OTHER, JUST LIKE MY STRING OF PEARLS

What different kinds of lines can we make?

THE SHORTEST DISTANCE BETWEEN TWO POINTS IS A STRAIGHT LINE

The Professor of Ideas asked the Professor of Form to hold on to one point and the Professor of Making to hold on to another and pull. Together they created a straight line. As it was formed, the Professor of Ideas explained, "The shortest distance between two points is a straight line."

AS A LINE BENDS AWAY FROM THE ORIGINAL POINT, IT BECOMES A CURVE

ACTIVITY

On a pin board, use two tacks to make two points. Connect them with a straight piece of string and then a curved piece of string. Next, take the two strings and measure them. Which piece is longer?

A CURVED LINE

The Professor of Ideas mischievously jumped like a tightrope walker onto the straight line held by the two professors. It bowed under her weight, bringing the middle of the line closer to the floor, and forming a curve.

As she balanced on the curved line, she said to the two professors, "The line of a curve bends away from the original point, stopping it from being straight."

Lesson 3

How do we make shapes out of lines?

The Professor of Form, who was holding some wool to create a line with the Professor of Making, decided he wanted to create a shape.

"There are three basic shapes I want to make today," he explained. "A triangle, a square, and a circle."

"To create a shape, we need to add more points and connect them together with more lines."

"So, to make a triangle, we need three points and three lines," he said.

Then he shuffled around and pointed to where his three other colleagues should stand to be of equal distance from each other.

"To make a square, we need four points connected by four lines of equal length."

"To make the final shape, which is a circle, we need to take away all the points," he said. The Professor of the Planet took one line, making the square corners round, and laid it down in a round shape on the studio floor.

"There," he said triumphantly. "We now have a circle."

ACTIVITY

Take four tacks (these are your points) and four pieces of string (these are your lines). Using a pin board, how many different kinds of shape can you create by joining together your points and lines?

SHAPES ARE CREATED WHEN POINTS ARE CONNECTED BY LINES TO CONTAIN SPACE

How do flat shapes become 3-D?

"The basic shapes that we have made until now from lines, such as the triangle, square, and circle, are flat," said the Professor of Form. "Flat shapes only have two dimensions: height and width." He made a square in the air using the wool to elaborate. "Height is the length from top to bottom, and width is the length from side to side."

Then the professor added some more points and lines to his square. "Notice how the flat shapes now appear to have space inside them? Shapes with volume have a third dimension: depth. Depth is the length from the front of an object to the back."

"By adding a third dimension—depth— to any flat shape, we can turn it into an object with volume," continued the Professor of Form. "We call these objects with volume 'three-dimensional,' or 3-D."

"Can we do this to any flat shape?" asked the Professor of the Planet.

"Yes!" replied the Professor of Form. "A circle can turn into a ball, or sphere, and a square can become a cube, like a dice. A triangle can become a cone, like an ice cream, if it has a circular base. And if a triangle has a square base, it can become a pyramid."

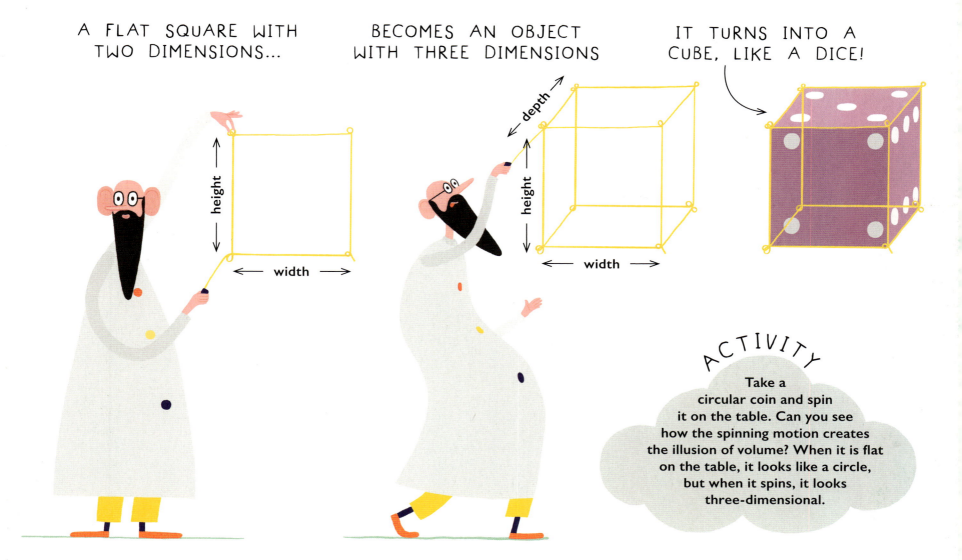

A FLAT SQUARE WITH TWO DIMENSIONS...

BECOMES AN OBJECT WITH THREE DIMENSIONS

IT TURNS INTO A CUBE, LIKE A DICE!

ACTIVITY

Take a circular coin and spin it on the table. Can you see how the spinning motion creates the illusion of volume? When it is flat on the table, it looks like a circle, but when it spins, it looks three-dimensional.

Lesson 5

What is on the outside of a shape?

A DICE IS A CUBE
AND HAS SIX SURFACES

AN OBJECT'S SURFACE
IS ITS OUTERMOST LAYER

The Professor of Form came into the room holding a dice.

"I want to talk to you about surfaces now," he said. "The surface of an object is its outermost layer—a bit like its shell. When an object has volume, it will have one or more surfaces."

"Look at this dice," he continued. "See how each side of the dice forms a surface, where the number of dots appear?"

The other professors nodded.

The Professor of Form held up the dice to demonstrate. "This cube has six surfaces, which we sometimes call 'planes.' Different objects have a different number of surfaces: a pyramid has five surfaces, while a sphere has only one surface. So, as we have seen, the volume of the cube is made up of its surfaces, lines, and points."

ACTIVITY

Around the house, can you find other three-dimensional objects to match the basic shapes: a pyramid for a triangle, a sphere for a circle, and a square for a cube? How many surfaces does each one have?

How does "tone" show us that something is 3-D?

The Professor of the Planet decided to show the other professors how light and shadow on an object's surfaces help to create tone. He took the group to the Greenhouse Studio, where light was streaming through the windows.

Tucked away among the lush green tropical forest of the Greenhouse Studio were sculptures of the basic shapes: a blue sphere, a red cube, and a yellow pyramid.

As it was late afternoon, the sun was low on the horizon. The Professor of the Planet pointed out the sculptures.

"See how the direction of the sunlight is creating shadows that wrap themselves around each of the forms?" he asked. He pointed to the side of the sphere where the sunlight created a small, bright spot of light, and where a fuzzy-edged, curved, dark shadow began.

"The effect of light and shadow creates tone: the junction where the lightness and the darkness meet."

The Professor of Ideas remarked, "It looks just like the Earth's moon, where the light creates daytime on one face of the moon, and on the other side it's nighttime in the shadow!"

"Yes, it does." The Professor of the Planet smiled.

"Tone is important because it allows us to see whether an object is flat (and therefore two-dimensional) or has volume (and is therefore three-dimensional)."

SUNLIGHT CREATES SHADOWS THAT WRAP THEMSELVES AROUND AN OBJECT TO CREATE TONE

SHADOW...

AND LIGHT HELP US SEE THAT AN OBJECT HAS VOLUME

ACTIVITY

Take a ball
and hold a light behind it.
Move the ball in front of the
light. Can you see how the shadows
change and give it tone? Try taking
three photos, each one showing the
ball with different shadows.

How do "shading" and "texture" make a drawing look more realistic?

The Professor of the Planet continued with his lesson about light, shade, and tone.

"Now, each of you draw a shape with volume," he said. "Look carefully at the sculptures of the cube, sphere, and pyramid, and try to show the different shadings of light and shadow in your drawing."

The professors started by drawing an outline of a square, circle, and triangle. As they had been shown in Lesson 4, they added extra lines to show depth. Then they filled in parts of the surfaces with different kinds of marks to show where the shadows fell. These marks changed the shapes from looking flat to looking 3-D.

"Crosshatch marks look like Twitter hashtags!" said the Professor of Ideas.

The Professor of the Planet smiled. "Yes, they do! Look carefully and you can see how the marks you have used make the shapes look 3-D. And they do something else, too."

"What else do these marks do?" asked the Professor of Making.

"The marks you have used create the effect of texture on the surfaces. Texture is how something feels when you touch it. Soft marks have given the Professor of Ideas' sphere a smooth texture. Scratchy marks have made the Professor of Senses' cube look as if it has a rough texture."

The professor looked at the drawings. "Now I can really imagine touching these objects!" he said. "They look more realistic."

TEXTURE SHOWS HOW A SURFACE WOULD FEEL IF YOU TOUCHED IT

ACTIVITY

Can you add crosshatch marks to a drawing of a circle so that it has volume and texture? Now your drawing should look like a 3-D ball, or sphere. Try the same thing with a pyramid and a cube.

Lesson 8

How do we create "patterns"?

SPOTS ARE A KIND OF PATTERN

ACTIVITY

Fold a piece of paper in half and cut out the shape of half a butterfly (with the body down the center fold). Open it up, then dip your thumb in some paint and create your own pattern on the butterfly's wings.

PATTERNS ARE CREATED BY THE SAME ELEMENTS, LIKE DOTS OR LINES, BEING REPEATED OVER AND OVER AGAIN

Next, the Professor of Making wanted to talk about pattern.

"Textures can also create patterns," she said. "What patterns can we see around us in the greenhouse?" she asked.

"What do you mean by pattern?" asked the Professor of Form.

The Professor of Making explained. "Patterns are created by the same elements, such as dots, splotches, or lines, being repeated several times or more. For example,

look above you. This monarch butterfly has a black, white, and orange pattern repeated on his wings."

"Many clothes have a patterned design, too," said the Professor of Making, "like the overalls I am wearing today."

The keen eyes of the Professor of Senses noticed that the Professor of Making was blending into the background.

"Look what is happening!" he said, and pointed to the Professor of Making's overalls,

designed with a repeated red-and-green floral motif. "She is merging into the bush behind her. We can hardly see her now!"

"I have seen this kind of pattern before," said the Professor of Ideas. "It confuses the eye and causes you to blend into your surroundings. It is called camouflage."

"Many animals in the wild, like cheetahs and zebras, are patterned like this to help them stay hidden" said the Professor of the Planet. "Isn't nature clever!"

CAMOUFLAGE IS A KIND OF PATTERN THAT CONFUSES THE EYE AND HELPS AN OBJECT BLEND INTO ITS SURROUNDINGS
STRIPES ARE A KIND OF PATTERN

How do we show "direction"?

BY SHOWING SOMEONE'S BODY IN
DIFFERENT POSITIONS AND SLANTED
AT DIFFERENT ANGLES, YOU CAN
SUGGEST THAT THEY ARE MOVING

Before moving on to the next lesson, the Professor of Senses quickly recapped what had been learned so far.

"In the Form Studio and Making Studio we learned about line, shape, form, and surface. In the Greenhouse Studio, the Professor of the Planet taught us about tone, light, shade, and texture. And the Professor of Making showed us how to look for pattern."

The professors nodded their heads in agreement. They had learned a lot!

"So far everything we have created looks static, as though it were fixed on the page and cannot move," said the Professor of Senses. "My question is: how can we create a way of showing movement, or visual direction, in our art?"

The Professor of Form thought about this for a moment, then said, "Look at me standing up very straight, and try to think of my body as a line." The Professor of Form held a stick to illustrate his point. "The line of my body is in a vertical direction, and so is this stick. My two feet are firmly on the ground and I won't fall over!"

Then the Professor of From began to lean at an angle, keeping his feet on the ground and the stick in a vertical position.

"Now I have moved my body into a slanted, or oblique, position," said the Professor of Form, "and the line of my body has a feeling of action and movement. Try some different positions yourselves," he instructed.

The Professor of the Planet nodded and curled up into a ball.

"Now my body forms a curved line," he said. "Do I also have a sense of movement?"

"Yes!" The Professor of Form smiled as the other professors joined in. "By showing your bodies in different positions and slanted at different angles, you each express a different sense of action."

ACTIVITY

On some grid paper, draw five stick people—one of them should be standing. Can you show that the other four stick men are moving by drawing them in different slanted and curved positions?

What is a color wheel?

PRIMARY COLORS
CANNOT BE MADE BY
MIXING OTHER COLORS,
WHEREAS SECONDARY
AND TERTIARY COLORS
ARE MIXED.

ACTIVITY

Make your own version of the color wheel showing the primary, secondary, and tertiary colors. Look in old magazines for pictures in the right colors, cut them out, and collage them together.

PRIMARY COLORS
ARE YELLOW, RED,
AND BLUE

"Today"—the Professor of Senses smiled— "we are going to explore color. To show how different colors are related, let's make a color wheel," he said.

The Professor of Making quickly reached for a paintbrush and began to draw out twelve pie-shaped wedges in a circle.

"There are three primary colors: yellow, red, and blue," said the Professor of Senses. The Professor of Making painted the three primary-colored sections on the wheel, with equal gaps of three between them.

"The primary colors are important because by mixing them together in different combinations, you can make all the other colors of the rainbow," continued the Professor of Senses.

"What about secondary colors?" asked the Professor of the Planet.

"By mixing two primary colors together, you can create a secondary color," explained the Professor of Senses. "The three secondary colors are orange, purple, and green."

The Professor of the Planet asked if he could add these to the color wheel. He mixed equal amounts of yellow and blue together to make green, and painted this into the segment in the middle of the two colors he had used.

"So green is half yellow and half blue— and sits midway between them on the color wheel," he observed.

"That's right!" said the Professor of Senses as the Professor of the Planet created purple from blue and red, and orange from red and yellow—painting these secondary colors into the middle segments.

"But what about the colors for the wedges between the primary and secondary colors?" asked the Professor of Form.

The Professor of Senses explained, "These are the tertiary colors. You can mix one primary color and one secondary color of equal amounts in order to create each of the six tertiary colors: yellow-orange, red-orange, red-purple, blue-purple, blue-green, and yellow-green."

The Professor of the Planet painted between the primary and secondary

SECONDARY COLORS

SECONDARY COLORS ARE ORANGE, PURPLE, AND GREEN

TERTIARY COLORS ARE YELLOW-ORANGE, RED-ORANGE, RED-PURPLE, BLUE-PURPLE, BLUE-GREEN, AND YELLOW-GREEN

TERTIARY COLORS

colors on the wheel, until all the wedges were filled.

The Professor of Senses smiled proudly. "This now gives us a twelve-part color wheel."

"Excellent!" exclaimed the professors, standing back to admire their work. "We've created the first School of Art color wheel!" The studio was suddenly awash with a rainbow of many different colors.

How do we make colors lighter and darker?

The Professor of Senses continued with his next lesson on color.

"The primary colors on the wheel are also called 'hues.' Hues are the purest colors—nothing has been added to them."

"What happens if you mix white paint into these colors?" asked the Professor of Making.

The Professor of Form squirted a dollop of bright white out of a paint tube and onto the yellow on his artist's palette. Mixing this up with his brush, he said, "Adding white to the original hue makes it lighter. Look at the pale yellow I have created."

"Yes," said the Professor of Senses. "This lighter color is called a 'tint.'"

"And what happens if you mix black paint into a color?" asked the Professor of Making.

"If you add black to a pure hue, it makes a darker version called a 'shade.'"

In order to demonstrate some of these effects, the Professor of Form added a tiny dab of black to the yellow. He saw that it created a much darker yellow color and recognized this as a "shade."

"Lastly," continued the Professor of Senses, "if you mix a dab of black and a dab of white

paint together, you will create a gray. If you add this gray to one of the pure hues, you will then get what we call a 'tone.'"

The Professor of Form added gray to the yellow, making a mustardy yellow color. He looked at the tints, shades, and tones that he had made and wrinkled up his nose in disapproval. He decided that he much preferred the primary yellow—especially as it was similar to the color of the middle button on his gray lab coat! This yellow was pure and strong, and looking at it made him feel happy.

ACTIVITY

Take a piece of paper and divide it into four. Choose a primary color and paint one of the squares this color. Then fill the other squares: the second square should be a tint, the third should be a shade, and the fourth should be a tone.

BY MIXING IN WHITE, YOU MAKE A LIGHTER COLOR, CALLED A TINT

BY MIXING IN BLACK, YOU MAKE A DARKER COLOR, CALLED A SHADE

BY MIXING IN GRAY, YOU MAKE ANOTHER COLOR, CALLED A TONE

How do colors work together in "harmony"?

The Professor of Senses decided to explore how the colors on the color wheel interacted with each other.

"Could you lay the wheel on the floor?" he asked. "Now, can three of you stand on segments next to each other?"

Three of the professors jumped onto three neighboring segments: blue-green, green, and yellow-green, while the Professor of the Planet hovered above them.

"How do you think these colors look together?" asked the Professor of Senses.

"They look nice," answered the Professor of the Planet. "The three colors work in harmony with each other."

"They remind me of the Professor of the Planet's plants!" said the Professor of Ideas.

Everyone thought about the colors in the Greenhouse Studio and how relaxing and pleasing they were to look at.

"Excellent!" said the Professor of Senses. "Groups of colors found next to each other on the color wheel are known as 'analogous' colors, and they work together in harmony."

"I can think of some other examples from nature," said the Professor of the Planet. "Are the oranges and reds of the leaves in autumn also analogous colors?"

"Yes!" said the Professor of Senses. "And so are the blues and blue-greens of the sky and the sea."

COLORS NEXT TO
EACH OTHER ON THE
COLOR WHEEL
ARE ANALOGOUS

ACTIVITY

Take a walk outside with your camera, and see if you can find some examples of harmonious colors in nature. What colors can you see at sunset? What colors are different leaves in a tree? Take a look!

How does "contrast" work to make colors brighter?

"Some colors look more brilliant when they are seen alongside another color," observed the Professor of Senses. "For example, the Professor of the Planet's yellow sweater looks extra bright against his purple trousers."

"That's true!" observed the Professor of Form.

"What do you notice about yellow and purple on the color wheel?" asked the Professor of Senses.

"Yellow is directly opposite purple!"

exclaimed the Professor of the Planet.

"Exactly," said the Professor of Senses. "Because they are opposite colors, they contrast with each other, which makes them appear brighter."

"Colors that sit opposite each other on the color wheel and contrast with each other in this way are called 'complementary' colors," said the Professor of Ideas. "This is because the secondary color complements, or enhances, the primary color, making it seem brighter. So, in the Professor of the Planet's

case, his top is yellow—a primary color— and his trousers are purple, which is the secondary color that sits opposite yellow on the color wheel."

"Well, thank you for the compliment about my complementary clothes!" said the Professor of the Planet, spinning in front of the color wheel, and everyone laughed.

ACTIVITY

Make your own piece of art by using contrasting colors! Draw the same object—like a shoe, or a flower—six times. Then color each drawing using every one of the six pairs of complementary colors on this wheel.

COMPLEMENTARY COLORS ARE FOUND OPPOSITE EACH OTHER ON THE COLOR WHEEL

Can we "see" colors that aren't there?

Not wanting to be outdone by the Professor of the Planet, the Professor of Form decided to show the others that on the inside of his lab coat was a special kind of color combination, too. He unbuttoned his jacket and opened it out.

"Look at the lining of my lab coat," he instructed the other professors. "What do you see?"

The Professor of Senses' eyes grew so large they nearly popped out of his head!

"I see a pattern of blue rectangles, yellow lines, and white circles—and, strangest of all, I see blue circles that seem to appear and disappear over the white circles!"

The other professors came up close to inspect this strange effect. From here they could see that the blue circles weren't there at all! It was just an illusion.

"But why do these ghostly dots appear?" asked the Professor of the Planet.

"The dots appear and disappear as your eye moves across the image. This happens because the part of your eye that processes light and dark gets confused by a complicated image made up of highly contrasting elements. So you see, your eyes don't always see exactly what is in front of them!" answered the Professor of Form with a wink and a nod.

YOUR EYES CAN BE FOOLED BY CERTAIN COLOR COMBINATIONS!

ACTIVITY

Create another illusion called an "afterimage." Paint a circle with three wedges—red, green, and blue—that meet in the middle. Take a long look directly at the center, then move your eyes to a white sheet of paper. What colors do you see now?

Does a color always look the same?

Still thinking about the last lesson, the Professor of Making took down her ladder (which was covered in red paint) and was carrying it back to her studio when she noticed something strange about its color. As she walked along the corridors, it seemed to look different against the contrasting walls: against the gray, the red was more vibrant; against the yellow, the red looked duller.

Looking more closely, she realized that the ladder's size also appeared to change a little against the different background colors. The ladder looked noticeably larger when it appeared against a gray corridor wall, and smaller against the yellow.

"Colors don't always look the same!" she said to herself. "The context you see them in can change their appearance!"

DIFFERENT BACKGROUNDS CAN APPEAR TO CHANGE A COLOR'S SIZE AND BRIGHTNESS

ACTIVITY

Try this
theory out for yourself!
Paint one piece of paper light
orange, and another gray. Next, paint
a small piece of paper a darker orange.
Does the smaller piece look browner next
to the lighter orange than it does
against the gray?

Lesson 16

Can different colors sometimes look the same?

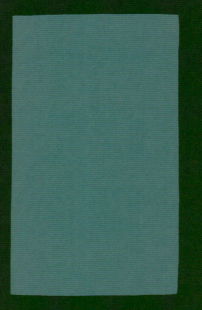

ACTIVITY

See if you can re-create this effect yourself. Try taking two shades of the same color and placing them against contrasting background colors. How does this affect their brightness and the size they appear?

TWO DIFFERENT
COLORS CAN BE
MADE TO LOOK
THE SAME

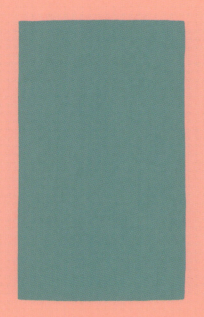

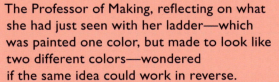

The Professor of Making, reflecting on what she had just seen with her ladder—which was painted one color, but made to look like two different colors—wondered if the same idea could work in reverse.

"Can my eyes be fooled into thinking that two different colors look like the same one?" she asked herself out loud. Just then, a door opened, and a friendly character she hadn't met before popped out.

"Hello! I am Professor Itten. The Professor of Form invited me here to talk about color with some of the students," he said, "and I couldn't help but overhear your question."

"And what do you think?" asked the Professor of Making. "Can two colors look like the same one?"

"Absolutely! Just look at these two windows!" he replied, and the Professor of Making saw that the two windows—both a different shade of blue—did indeed look the same color. But when she saw the colors side by side on the doors, the difference between the colors was obvious.

Can color affect how you are feeling?

It was the last lesson of the term, and the Professor of Senses was thinking back over what they had learned about color. He remembered the Professor of Form talking about how the color yellow made him happy, and he remembered feeling calm when discussing the blues and blue-greens of the sky and sea. He liked how the Professor of the Planet's shirt and trousers were designed in complementary colors and became more vibrant due to contrast.

Then he thought about the analogous colors on the color wheel, and remembered that they were very similar to those in the Professor of the Planet's Greenhouse Studio, where the natural colors were relaxing because they were perfectly harmonious.

Color, he decided, had many different meanings and associations, and could cause you to experience different emotions. He supposed that how you felt about different colors depended on your background, experiences, culture, and education. Perhaps that was why everybody has a different favorite color! he thought.

DIFFERENT COLOR COMBINATIONS CAN CAUSE DIFFERENT REACTIONS

ACTIVITY

Try this theory out for yourself. Paint a picture of two rooms—one bright yellow, the other one blue. Ask ten people which room looks happy, and which makes them feel calm. What do they say?

YELLOW CAN
MAKE SOME
PEOPLE
FEEL HAPPY

ANALOGOUS
COLORS CREATE
A HARMONIOUS
ENVIRONMENT

CONTRASTING
COLORS
LOOK GOOD
TOGETHER

What design principles help us to make art?

Now we have learned about the basic design elements, we are ready to think about the basic design principles. But what are these? That is what we are going to discover this term!

Imagine baking a sponge cake. You have a set of ingredients: flour, sugar, butter, eggs, and milk, which you mix together in a particular way before you put them into a cake pan, then into the oven to cook. Later, you take the cake out, cool it, and add the icing—and perhaps some sprinkles!

The process of baking a cake is similar to how we might create a design or an artwork. You take ingredients (the basic elements) and by mixing them together, using the principles you have learned, you create an object. Principles are the rules and ideas that artists and designers use to structure basic elements and make art.

We learned in the first term that basic design elements are the things that we could use to create works in art and design. As we start the second term at the School of Art, you will be introduced to basic design principles and explore how they might work. These principles form a kind of artist's tool kit, which will equip you with balance, movement, repetition, contrast, proportion, rhythm, and symmetry. By using these tools, you will find it easier to express yourself and present your work in an interesting way.

This chapter is divided into two general areas: composition and relationships. You will be introduced to specific ways of using the basic elements and how to organize or position them. We begin with the Professor of Form, who introduces us to the grid, which he uses to move the basic design elements around in particular way to make a composition. Experiment with this yourself, and have fun playing with perspective, proportion, negative and positive space, and visual weight.

Later you will explore a set of visual relationships and discover why a composition might feel balanced—or unbalanced! Learn about what weight "looks" like, and see what happens to the Professor of Ideas when she finds herself in an unbalanced composition—*wheeee!*

The natural environment is a good place to learn about balance, too. The Professor of the Planet's monarch butterfly shows us how symmetry is created in nature through pattern. And what appears in nature can be replicated in art—which the Professor of Making shows us by drawing on her tablet to explore the principle of asymmetry. Can you guess what asymmetry might look like?

We will learn how, by changing an element's size and color, you can make it more attention-grabbing than other elements. And what if you want to bring order to your composition? Check out Lesson 30 on alignment, which shows you how to use a grid to visually connect elements.

Our term ends by exploring repetition and movement. Find out what happens when the Professor of Senses turns on his dance music to demonstrate the relationship between musical and visual rhythms. The principle of movement is explored by revisiting what we learned about direction in the first term. Now the professors want to know how visual direction impacts how the viewer's eye might move across a composition.

Now we have all of the ingredients to bake our cake. It is time to get to grips with the basic principles of design. There's lots to look forward to this term—see you there!

Lesson 18

What is a "grid"?

A GRID'S EQUALLY SPACED, CRISSCROSSED LINES HELP ARTISTS TO ORGANIZE THE ELEMENTS IN THEIR ARTWORK

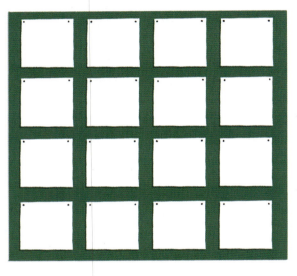

A GRID IS MADE UP OF EQUAL-SIZED SQUARES

ACTIVITY

Draw a square 6 inches high and 6 inches wide. Fill it with horizontal lines a half inch apart, and vertical lines a half inch apart. This is your grid! How many squares can you count?

The Professor of Form decided it was time to take what they knew about the basic elements and see what would happen when they introduced a set of basic design principles. He invited everyone to his studio.

"Tell me," he asked, "what do you notice about the way I have decorated the walls and floor of my studio?"

All the professors looked quizzically around the room, and the Professor of Making answered, "Your studio has been divided into squares with a series of white lines."

"It is one large grid!" exclaimed the Professor of Ideas. They all looked around, and indeed, white lines were drawn all over the room, equally dividing the floor, walls, and ceiling into squares of the same size.

Every square was made up of straight vertical and horizontal lines. Each professor walked over to one of the squares and stood in the middle of it.

"The grid," explained the Professor of Form, "provides you, the artist, with a framework to organize the different basic elements we have learned about. It allows you to think about the structure of your work more easily," he said.

What does "composition" mean in art?

IN A FORMAL
STRUCTURE, THINGS
ARE ARRANGED IN
AN ORDERLY WAY

"Can you please show us what 'structure' means?" asked the Professor of Ideas.

"Of course!" replied the Professor of Form. He motioned to the four professors to stand in the corners of the nine-square grid on the floor. Each of them stood in the center of their square unit, meaning they were an equal distance from each other.

"Now you are standing in a formal structure," said the Professor of Form. "This is created by placing yourselves the same distance apart on the grid. There is a similarity to the spacing between you and your neighbors, and this gives you a sense of visual stability. Everything looks organized, controlled, and orderly," he said with an approving nod.

The Professor of Form motioned to the professors to rearrange themselves. This time he instructed them to stand wherever they wanted to.

"Perfect!" said the Professor of Form, standing back from the grid. As he had anticipated, they looked very disorganized now! "You have now placed yourself in an informal structure, where the group is not arranged in a recognizable pattern.

COMPOSITION IS THE WAY IN WHICH THINGS ARE BROUGHT TOGETHER AND ARRANGED

ACTIVITY

Using your grid from Lesson 18, choose four items and arrange them in a formal structure, equal distances apart. Next, rearrange them in an informal structure, placing them anywhere. Which design looks more organized?

You are not an equal distance from each other on the grid, which gives you a sense of visual instability. Things look unorganized and disorderly." The Professor of Form sniffed. He liked things just so.

Now the professors began to understand the importance of the grid.

"I've heard of 'composition,'" said the Professor of Ideas. "Does structure have anything to do with this?" she asked.

"Yes!" said the Professor of Form. "Composition is the way in which things are brought together and arranged. Both formal structures and informal structures are kinds of composition— they are different ways of arranging things."

IN AN INFORMAL STRUCTURE, THINGS ARE ARRANGED IN A DISORDERLY WAY

How does "perspective" work?

PERSPECTIVE CAUSES
THINGS TO APPEAR SMALLER
AS THEY MOVE INTO THE
DISTANCE, WHICH CREATES
A SENSE OF DEPTH

IN THE FOREGROUND, THE
SPACE CLOSEST
TO THE VIEWER, THINGS
APPEAR BIGGER

IN THE BACKGROUND,
THE SPACE FARTHEST
FROM THE VIEWER, THINGS
APPEAR SMALLER

The Professor of Form decided to explore a new design principle while everyone was still standing on the grid: perspective. He asked the Professor of Senses to stand next to him on one of the squares closest to the group. "The Professor of Senses and I are both standing in the foreground, near to you, the viewers. What do you notice about my size compared to the Professor of Senses?" he asked.

"You are taller than the Professor of Senses," observed the Professor of Making.

"Correct!" said the Professor of Form.

Then he moved two squares backward, so that he was farther away from the viewers.

"Now what do you notice about my size compared to the Professor of Senses?" he called from the back of the room.

The other professors gasped.

"You look smaller than him!" said the Professor of Making.

"Correct!" said the Professor of Form. "Now I am standing farther away, I appear smaller. I haven't actually shrunk; this has to do with perspective. The farther away things are, the smaller they seem."

"Why is that?" asked the Professor of Senses.

"Is this connected to scale?" asked the Professor of Ideas.

"Yes!" replied the Professor of Form. "'Scale' is about the relationship between one object and another. When we stand side by side, you and I are the same scale, but as I move backward, our relative scale changes and I appear smaller than you."

The professors nodded—now they understood perspective better.

ACTIVITY

Take a series of photos with your friends. Try changing the perspective in each photograph—making yourselves seem smaller or larger in relation to each other—by moving into the foreground or background.

What does it mean when we say something is in "proportion"?

Draw a simple face with two eyes, two ears, a nose, and a mouth. Draw another outline of a face at the same size, but draw the eyes smaller and the ears bigger. Which face looks out of proportion to you?

WHEN EVERYTHING IS THE RIGHT SIZE RELATIVE TO ITS SURROUNDINGS, IT IS SAID TO BE IN PROPORTION

The Professor of Senses decided now would be a good time to talk about the principle of proportion, which he understood best of all.

"When we talk about proportion, we are looking at the size of each part in relation to the whole."

This sounded perplexing to the other professors, but the Professor of Senses smiled.

"Look at my face," he instructed. "Each of the different parts—my ears, my nose, my chin, and so on—are positioned in relation to one another. The comparison of size between the different features and their distance from one another is called proportion. When everything seems to be in the right position and the right size, this creates visual harmony, and we can say that everything looks in proportion."

The Professor of Senses pointed at his nose. He sniffed and it began to grow bigger. Then, with a wiggle, so did his ears.

"Now, see how the relationship between the size of my eyes and nose has changed, compared to the rest of my face. Don't I look strange?" he asked, and the other professors giggled.

"My nose and ears are out of proportion with the rest of my face!" he explained.

Then he flexed his fingers and his hands grew. "And now my hands are out of proportion to my body!" he added, and flapped them comically.

How do we draw realistic human proportions?

Test this theory for yourself! With a friend, measure your arm span, from fingertip to fingertip, and your height from head to toe. Are the two lengths almost the same?

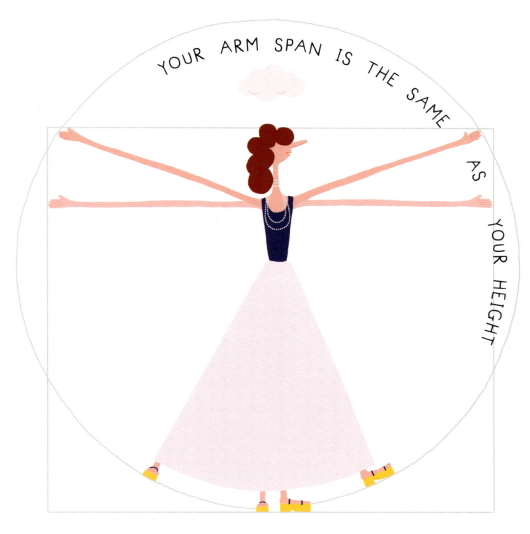

YOUR ARM SPAN IS THE SAME AS YOUR HEIGHT

While they were on the subject of proportion, the Professor of Ideas suddenly thought about a picture by Leonardo da Vinci called *Vitruvian Man*.

"It shows the correct proportions of a person, and you can use it if you want to create a realistic image of a human," said the Professor of Ideas.

"Da Vinci was an artist and scientist who had lived more than 500 years ago,"

she continued. "But let's see if we can re-create his diagram now!"

She lay on the floor and stretched out her arms and legs. She asked the Professor of Form to draw a perfect circle around her.

Then, keeping her head in the same place, she moved her legs straight down and her arms straight out. She asked the Professor of Form to draw a square around her.

"What do we know about squares?" asked the Professor of Ideas.

"Squares have the same height and width," answered the Professor of Making.

"So, if my body perfectly fits inside a square, what does that mean about my proportions?" she asked.

"You also have the same height and width! Your arm span has the same measurement as your height!" said the Professor of Making.

"Correct!" The Professor of Ideas beamed.

How do we make a "silhouette"?

A SILHOUETTE IS A SIMPLE
BLACK-AND-WHITE PORTRAIT,
MADE OF POSITIVE
AND NEGATIVE SPACE

"Now that we have thought about scale and proportion, let's draw some simple portraits," announced the Professor of Ideas.

"Your first step is to take your marker and draw in outline a profile of one of your colleagues. Your profile is how your face looks side-on," she added. The professors scurried around getting ready.

"Take your pen and start drawing from the top of the head, down the forehead to the ridge of the nose, around the end of the nose, then over the lips and down the chin. Keep going until you reach the chest.

Remember Lesson 22 on proportion, and carefully depict the distance between each part of the face to be as accurate as possible."

All of the professors started drawing, including the Professor of Ideas, whose subject was the Professor of Form.

"Now, to continue," the Professor of Making said, taking the lead, "use your black marker to fill in the profile portrait. Be careful not to go over the outline that you have just drawn."

As the professors did this, they noticed that soon half the page was white and the

other half, inside their professor's profile, was black.

"Well done! You have each created a silhouette!" said the Professor of Making. "We can also talk about your picture in terms of what we see as 'positive space' and 'negative space.' The drawing of the professor makes up positive space, while the white area around the drawing makes up negative space. Note how you need both positive and negative space to see the professor's profile clearly!"

ACTIVITY

Create a silhouette of a friend by carefully drawing an outline of their profile. Then fill in the head shape with black (this is the positive space) and leave the background white (this is the negative space).

THE BLACK AREA
FORMS THE POSITIVE SPACE

THE WHITE AREA FORMS THE NEGATIVE SPACE

What do we mean when we say things look "light" and "heavy"?

The next day the Professor of Ideas called everyone into her studio, as she wanted to demonstrate the idea of visual "weight."

"I want us to think about what 'light' and 'heavy' both look like," she said as the professors came through the door. "Now, what do you make of the clouds in my room?" she asked.

"They look light and fluffy, just like real clouds!" answered the Professor of Senses.

"And what makes them look light?" asked the Professor of Ideas.

"Well, they are a light color," replied the Professor of Senses thoughtfully, "and they have soft edges, which helps them blend in with their surroundings."

"Very good!" said the Professor of Ideas. The Professor of the Planet floated up into the air to touch one of the clouds, and the Professor of Ideas, who was in a mischievous mood, pulled out a large blue sphere that the Professor of Making had brought her as a gift.

"What about this sphere?" she asked. "Does this look light or heavy?"

"That looks heavy to me," answered the Professor of the Planet. "It is a dark color, has a hard shape, and contrasts with its surroundings. It stands out in your light and airy studio."

"Yes," said the Professor of Ideas, who nevertheless seemed to hold it effortlessly.

"Do you want to see if you are right?" she asked, offering him the sphere. The Professor of the Planet reached out to hold it, and, feeling its weight, crashed to the studio floor.

"You were right!" said the Professor of Ideas with a giggle as the Professor of the Planet dusted himself down. "This blue sphere is heavy—and it looks heavy, too. It has visual weight, which draws our attention to it."

ACTIVITY

Test this theory! Take a pack of white mints, and spill them on a plate. Then add a chocolate to the group. Draw what you see, and afterward, ask people what their eye is drawn to. What do they say?

THINGS WITH VISUAL WEIGHT DRAW OUR ATTENTION IN A SCENE

HEAVY THINGS (WITH VISUAL
WEIGHT) ARE OFTEN DARK
AND CONTRAST WITH THEIR
LIGHT SURROUNDINGS

What do we mean when we talk about "balance" in art?

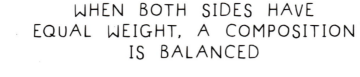

ACTIVITY

Take your grid from Lesson 18. Draw a line down the middle of the page and arrange four coins on it—two on each side of the line. Now try taking away one of the coins. Which composition feels more balanced?

WHEN BOTH SIDES HAVE EQUAL WEIGHT, A COMPOSITION IS BALANCED

Once the professors had begun to understand weight, the Professor of Form decided it was time to talk about balance.

"I have brought a few of my basic shapes here to help in our next lesson," he announced.

Reaching into the box, the Professor of Ideas pulled out a large yellow triangle and a long, straight red plank of wood, which she placed on top of the triangle.

"Right," said the Professor of Form. "I need one of us to sit on either end of the red plank. To make it balance, we need to be the same weight."

"It's like a seesaw!" said the Professor of Making, while the Professor of Senses jumped on the plank opposite the Professor of Form. After a brief wobble, they became stable, their legs dangling in the air. Because

they were of equal weight, they were able to balance on the plank so it didn't tip.

"Now it's my turn," said the Professor of Ideas, who carefully replaced the Professor of Form on one end of the wooden plank. Before anyone could speak, the Professor of Ideas—whose slight body was much lighter than the Professor of Senses'—was catapulted into the air! The

WHEN EITHER SIDE ARE
DIFFERENT WEIGHTS, A
COMPOSITION IS UNBALANCED

Professor of the Planet roared with laughter as the Professor of Ideas landed with a bump on one of the clouds floating in her studio.

"See how important balance is!" the Professor of Form said. "You need to have equal weight on either side to achieve balance, and it is the same when you are making art. If your design has too much weight on one side, it feels unbalanced."

"I've got an idea!" said the Professor of the Planet, beckoning to the Professor of Ideas. She jumped down off her cloud and together they equaled out the weight of the Professor of Senses. The plank became horizontal again, with the weight evenly distributed.

"Very clever!" said the Professor of Form.

"When you have something very heavy, you have to balance it out with lots of light things."

"Well, I think we all understand balance well enough now!" said the Professor of Senses, looking a bit cross, and everybody smiled.

What is "symmetry"?

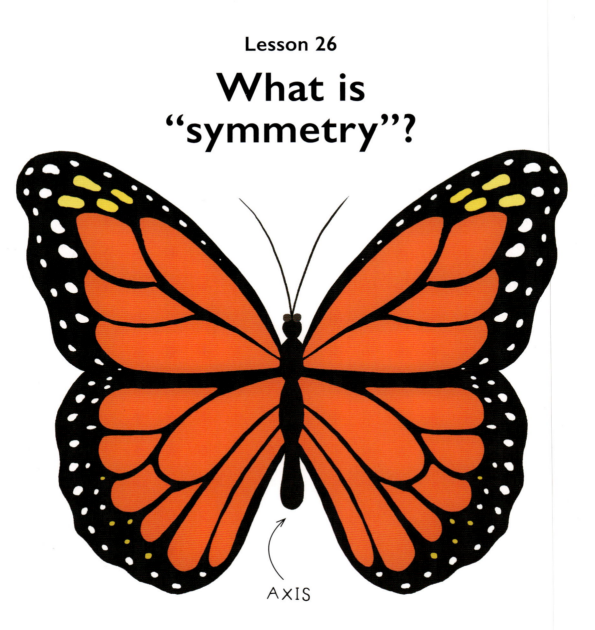

AXIS

THE BUTTERFLY'S WINGS PERFECTLY MIRROR
EACH OTHER ON EITHER SIDE OF
THE BODY, WHICH FORMS THE CENTRAL
AXIS—THIS MAKES IT SYMMETRICAL

The Professor of Making knew that if the professors understood balance, then they would also understand the basic principle of symmetry. As she was pondering how to demonstrate this idea, she looked up and noticed a monarch butterfly from the Professor of the Planet's Greenhouse Studio. It gracefully flew around her head, and she noticed its stunning orange-and-black pattern. She saw that both wings were exactly the same: a perfect mirror image of each other. As it flew, its body formed a central axis, from which both of the wings folded. The way the butterfly's wings mirrored each other made it symmetrical. But also, the butterfly's symmetry made it perfectly balanced. This simple organization made the butterfly look beautiful. The Professor of Making explained all this to the others.

ACTIVITY

Make your own symmetrical drawing. Fold a sheet of paper in half. On either side, can you draw a symmetrical pattern? Try counting the number of squares you use on both sides to help you make a mirror image.

What is "asymmetry"?

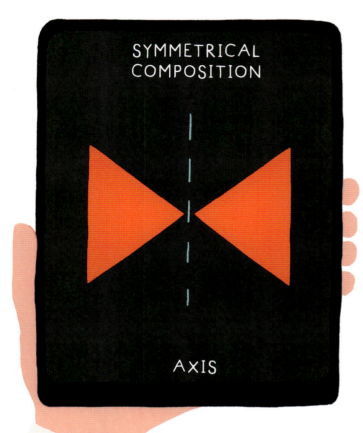

IN THIS SYMMETRICAL DESIGN, THE ELEMENTS ARE MIRRORED ON EITHER SIDE OF THE CENTRAL AXIS

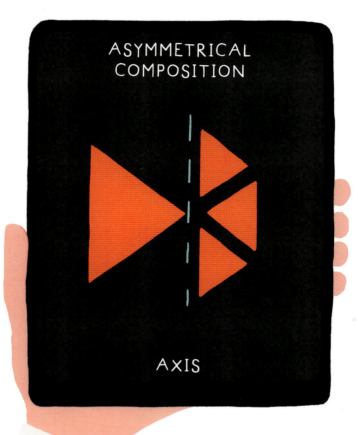

IN THIS ASYMMETRICAL DESIGN, THE ELEMENTS AREN'T MIRRORED BUT ARE STILL VISUALLY BALANCED

The Professor of Making then asked, "Does anyone know what 'asymmetrical' means?"

"Well, if symmetry is about order, asymmetry is about disorder, but in a good way. If you put elements together in a less organized way, you can draw attention to interesting parts of your composition," replied the Professor of Ideas.

"Does this mean that the weight on either side of the axis must be different?" asked the Professor of Form.

"Not always," replied the Professor of Ideas. "The visual weight can be balanced, even if the elements are different."

To help explain, the Professor of Making pulled out her tablet and drew one large triangle on half of the screen, then three small triangles of equal size on the other side of the screen. The design was asymmetrical, but the visual weight was still balanced.

ACTIVITY

Try drawing two kinds of bicycles: the first, a modern one, and the second, a penny-farthing. Which one is basically symmetrical, and which is asymmetric (with differently sized wheels)?

In what different ways can things "contrast"?

"Now it's time to think about contrast again," said the Professor of Form. "Come with me back to my studio and let's see what we can use to show how contrast works!"

All the professors followed him and watched him pull down from a shelf one large orange triangle and one small blue circle.

"Okay, let's place these on the grid." The Professor of Form carefully positioned the small blue circle on one side of the central grid line, which became the axis, and the large orange triangle on the other.

"The way I have placed this blue circle and orange triangle on either side of a central axis makes this composition asymmetrical because of their contrasting sizes," said the Professor of Form.

"But the big size of the triangle and the small size of the circle aren't the only ways in which these two things contrast," added the Professor of Form. "What else do you notice?"

"Well, the triangle is orange and the circle is blue and these colors contrast with each other," said the Professor of the Planet, thinking about Lesson 13.

"Spot on!" said the Professor of Form.

THESE TWO ELEMENTS CONTRAST IN SIZE ONLY

THE MORE WAYS IN
WHICH TWO ELEMENTS
CONTRAST, THE MORE
OBVIOUS THEIR
DIFFERENCE BECOMES

ACTIVITY

Look around the house, and see if you can collect objects that contrast in size only, in color only, and in shape only. Then look for two things that contrast in size, color, *and* shape. Can you draw each pair?

THESE TWO ELEMENTS CONTRAST
IN SIZE, COLOR, AND SHAPE,
WHICH MAKES THEIR
DIFFERENCE MORE OBVIOUS

"These colors appear opposite each other on the color wheel, and so they are in contrast with each other. Do you notice anything else?"

The Professor of Senses' hands grew bigger as he thought about how the shapes felt.

"The blue circle is smooth and round, while the orange triangle cube has straight edges and pointy corners," he answered.

"That's true," said the Professor of Form, "that is another way in which they contrast."

The Professor of the Planet, floating over, added, "I feel different emotions when I look at these two shapes. The roundness of the circle is smooth, for example, and gives me a feeling of comfort. The color blue makes me feel calm. On the other hand, the orange triangle's sharp edges and bright orange color have more energy.

It makes me feel happy to look at it. Is that another kind of contrast?"

"Yes!" said the Professor of Form. "All of the things you have observed are correct—there are lots of ways in which the two shapes contrast. And the greater the contrast between two elements, the more obvious the difference."

How does "hierarchy" affect what you look at?

Next the Professor of Making wanted to tackle the principle of hierarchy.

She had seen that when two elements—like the blue circle and orange triangle—were placed next to each other, the larger element appeared to have more visual weight, and became more eye-catching because of its size, color, and placement.

To talk about hierarchy with the other professors, she asked the Professor of Form for a large yellow square and the small blue circle. When she placed them on the grid, the small blue circle seemed to move into the background, while the larger yellow square appeared closer and in the foreground.

"Which of these two shapes grabs your attention more?" she asked.

"The square," replied the Professor of Form.

"And what is it about the square that catches your eye?" she asked again.

"Well, it's a lighter color and bigger than the circle," said the Professor of Form.

"Yes!" answered the Professor of Making. "These things make it more prominent in the composition. You are drawn to look at the yellow square because it appears lighter and closer to you. This is how hierarchy works: it causes your eye to rank all of the elements in a composition according to their visual importance. The attention-grabbing elements—like the yellow square—are higher in the hierarchy than the other elements, like the blue circle, and so you look at them first."

The Professor of Form nodded, as he found it to be true.

"As we saw in our earlier lessons, you can apply this principle by altering an element's size and color, and by using its visual weight. Visual hierarchies like this help to organize and emphasize the importance of one element over another, and show you where to start when you look at a piece of art."

VISUAL HIERARCHY CAUSES YOU
TO NOTICE THE LARGER, LIGHTER
ELEMENTS IN THE FOREGROUND
BEFORE YOU LOOK AT OTHER
ELEMENTS IN THE BACKGROUND

ACTIVITY

Test this
for yourself!
Create your own
composition using a large yellow
square, a small blue circle, and some
small gray triangles. Ask your friends
which object they look at most. Is it
the large yellow square?

LARGE, LIGHT OBJECTS IN
THE FOREGROUND
DRAW YOUR ATTENTION MORE...

THAN SMALL DARK
ELEMENTS IN THE
BACKGROUND

How does "alignment" bring order to your composition?

THESE ELEMENTS ARE
ALIGNED HORIZONTALLY
ALONG THE BASELINE

The Professor of Form pulled out a large pad of paper with a grid drawn on it, and an orange marker.

"One way to help visually organize a composition of different elements is through alignment. Let me show you what I mean," said the professor, and began to draw a series of three triangles on one of the sheets of grid paper.

He drew the bottom of each triangle on the same horizontal grid baseline, so that the elements were in a straight line, positioned one after another.

Then, on another piece of paper, the professor drew three different-sized rectangles—one large, one medium, and one small. Even though they were varied sizes, the left-hand edge of each

rectangle touched the same vertical grid line, forming a straight line. Visually this looked nice and orderly.

"Alignment means that each element is lined up with the others, so they are on the same line of sight. In other words, you can draw a straight line from one end to the other and the elements are visually connected."

THESE ELEMENTS ARE ALIGNED ALONG A VERTICAL LINE

ACTIVITY

Take your sketchbook or a camera and look for examples of things in alignment in your daily life, for instance, books on a shelf, or crayons in a pack. Do you like the orderly effect this creates?

Lesson 31

What does "repetition" look like?

The Professor of Senses decided to take the others to his studio for the last lessons of the day and asked the Professor of Form to bring his pad of grid paper, set of markers, and bag of basic elements with him.

As the professors entered, it was clear that the Professor of Senses had been keeping his greatest passion a secret all year: dance music. Blaring out of some huge speakers was a dance beat—the repetitive drum and bass rhythm shook the objects on the table. All the professors found themselves nodding and tapping their feet as the music played. The Professor of

Senses' ears grew even larger as he enjoyed the sensation of listening to one of his favorite tunes.

He turned down the music a bit and shouted, "Can you hear the repetition of the drumbeat?"

"Yes!" cried back the group, who could hear the drumbeat being repeated over and over again.

"Clap along!" he said and, as they did, he explained, "This drumbeat creates a recurring sound pattern over time, just like your claps."

To explain how this principle could

work visually, he decided to show what repetition looked like. He asked the Professor of Form for a handful of cone shapes and told him to line them up on the floor.

"Look at these cones," said the Professor of Senses. "They are the same kind of element, placed equal distances apart. Can you see how they cause visual repetition, just like the drumbeat?"

"Yes!" shouted back the other professors, and the Professor of Senses turned the music up again as loudly as he could.

ACTIVITY

Go to your local library and ask for a book on Andy Warhol, an American artist. Look at his paintings of common objects, such as soup cans, and famous people. How does he use repetition in his art? Make your own artwork, inspired by this artist.

BY USING THE SAME ELEMENTS AND PLACING THEM EQUAL DISTANCES APART, YOU CREATE REPETITION

What is "rhythm" in art ?

After another minute or two of the deafening music, the Professor of Senses turned it down a little and yelled, "Can you hear that when the bass guitar and the voice of the singer come in, this combination of sounds creates a rhythm?"

"Yes!" shouted back the professors.

"Let's create our own rhythm!" cried the Professor of Senses. "I need your help!"

The Professor of Ideas took off her pearls and lined up the beads, each of which was repeated in a regular pattern along the strand.

The Professor of the Planet thought about the repeated patterns made by nature, like the repeated stripes on a zebra, and began to draw on a piece of paper.

The Professor of Senses took the Professor of Ideas' pearls and the Professor of the Planet's drawings, along with the cones from earlier, and used them to create a rhythm. To start with, it looked less regular than the repeated cones, but over time a visual rhythm began to emerge. Because of the different elements, it looked more vibrant than the repeated cones from before.

"Can you see what rhythm looks like now?" he shouted to the other professors, and they all waved their arms in agreement.

ACTIVITY

Look up the work of the artist Bridget Riley on the internet. Choose one of her paintings to look at. How does your eye move across the painting? What patterns are there? What elements are repeated? Can you find rhythm in her work?

BY ALTERNATING THE ELEMENTS AND PLACING THEM EQUAL DISTANCES APART, YOU CREATE RHYTHM

How do repetition, rhythm, and pattern create visual movement?

It was the final lesson of term. Before the holidays, the professors wanted to learn how repetition, pattern, and rhythm might make the viewer's eyes move across a composition.

The Professor of Senses, still dancing away to his music, announced to the others, "When I dance, I am creating movement. As I listen to the music, the rhythm makes my body move from side to side, and I move up and down the studio!" He gave a little wiggle to illustrate his point. "It works the same way in an artwork. If we are clever, we can position elements in different ways to create a sense of rhythm, which makes our eyes move across a composition."

"Let's try this out!" said the Professor of Ideas, who was intrigued by his explanation. "First up, let's create rhythm with a series of triangles. Make sure they are equally spaced, and align them (like we did in Lesson 30). Now, what happens when you look at them?"

"The regular spacing makes my eye move from one end of the line to the other," replied the Professor of Senses.

"Indeed!" continued the Professor of Ideas. "Now, this time, let's alternate each triangle with a zebra print! This creates a different kind of visual rhythm as our eye is pulled from one shape to the other, from the start to the finish of the line."

"Yes, I see!" said the Professor of Senses. "This is a bit like Lesson 32, on creating a

visual rhythm. Can I borrow your pearls? With these, we can create a line, which shows what movement looks like! Our eyes will follow this line through the composition."

"Lastly, for fun," said the Professor of Ideas, "let's draw the triangles and zebra prints with different distances between them. Use the pearls again to map your eye movement across the page. See how dynamic the composition becomes?"

The professors were happy that they now understood how the basic elements and design principles could be used. What they wanted to know next was how did all these lessons apply to the world outside the School of Art?

ACTIVITY

Follow the professors and try drawing different kinds of visual movement. Try different variations on the same theme. Remember how these principles can help the viewer move through your composition as they look at it.

THE EQUAL SPACING OF THE
TRIANGLES MAKES YOUR EYE MOVE
FROM ONE END OF THE LINE
TO THE OTHER

ALTERNATING THE TRIANGLES AND
ZEBRA PRINTS PULLS YOUR EYE FROM
ONE SHAPE TO ANOTHER, IN A WAVE

PLACING THE TRIANGLES
AND ZEBRA PRINTS AT DIFFERENT
DISTANCES MAKES YOUR EYE
MOVEMENT MORE DYNAMIC

What can you do with your newfound skills?

As the professors of the School of Art, we like to make sure that our ideas reach out to different people in different places. While it is perfectly fine to make things because we want to, we also feel it is important to contribute our creative skills and ideas to make the world a better place. Today, lots of artists and designers are working with scientists, medical professionals, environmentalists, psychologists, and others to help make a better future.

We are all citizens in a global society and need to help each other when we can. But we know that we can't resolve all the problems in the world by ourselves! So, the best way to make a difference is to begin thinking about how you can address issues close to home.

In our third term, you will find out how our senses help us understand our environment, and how we can use them to help us think visually. Making your ideas visual—for instance, by drawing them—can help you think a problem through more clearly.

Your newfound skills might also help you communicate ideas to your friends, perhaps, telling stories using pictures. Comic books are a fun and effective way to do this. You can tell a story frame by frame—and if you want it to, your story can carry an environmental message, or get across other important information. The same can be said for creating an infographic, which packages up facts and makes them interesting to look at and easy to understand.

Stories can be used to help explain complex ideas. With so much data available today, we need to find ways of making sense of this information. By using art and design to communicate facts, we can help others make decisions about how to live their lives. See how the Professor of Making spurs the School of Art on to become more energy efficient in Lesson 37.

As professors and students, we encounter design challenges every day, often in our own homes. Take, for example, the importance of reusing and recycling plastic. We know that plastic bottles and plastic bags are not good for the environment. So how can we use our newfound skills to create new uses for plastic bags? Join us as we think about different ways to recycle—we're sure you have some good ideas!

Sharing ideas with others is also important. In the School of Art, we like to share what we have learned in our lessons in order to hear other people's opinions. By working with other people—something we sometimes call co-creation—we can find new and exciting ways of solving issues together.

One of the most important things you will learn in the School of Art is the value of experimentation. Most of all, we want to encourage you to have the confidence to try new things and to push your ideas. We suggest you keep a sketchbook of all the things you're learning about, drawings of what you've seen, and ideas for future projects. Don't worry about making mistakes. In art, there are no mistakes—only unexpected outcomes!

This brings us to the last lesson of the year in the School of Art. If you have learned to use basic design elements and principles well, then the way in which you put everything together will have what we call an "aesthetic," which means it will be pleasing to our senses.

We know our world is changing, and the future holds many challenges. Now is the time for you to make a difference using your newly acquired skills!

How can we think visually?

VISUALS, LIKE MAPS, HELP YOU TO THINK THROUGH A PROBLEM

ACTIVITY

Draw a visual map of your own journey from home to school. Include details of any landmarks that activate your senses: do you pass any places with distinctive sounds or smells, like a bakery, or memorable sights?

The new term was off to a good start! Thinking back on all they had learned so far, the Professor of Senses reflected, "It is good to have new skills, but how do we show what we have learned? How can we apply our new skills to the wider world?"

"We could start off close to home," said the Professor of Ideas. "What if we could discover ways of helping each other and the community around the school?"

The professors liked this idea.

"But before we do this, we need to look at ways we can communicate our ideas so that people can understand them better," continued the Professor of Ideas.

"Do you use your senses to think visually?" she asked.

The professors looked confused.

"Take, for example, my cat," continued the Professor of Ideas, pointing to Fluffy. "How do you think Fluffy knows how to get to her dinner in the School of Art's corridor? She uses her senses, which help her to visualize how to find it. For example, her whiskers help her work out how small a space is and whether she can crawl through it on her way there. Her eyesight helps her as she scurries down the corridor, and her sense of smell helps her track down her dinner."

"Let's create a plan for Fluffy, called a visual, to think through the fastest journey she can take to find her dinner," said the Professor of Senses. Together they mapped routes through the school, making sure to include the sensory details, like sounds and smells, they associated with different spots.

"Visuals like this are a useful way to think through alternative solutions. See here— we've come up with three routes. Which one is the most direct route?" asked the Professor of Senses, and the others tried to decide.

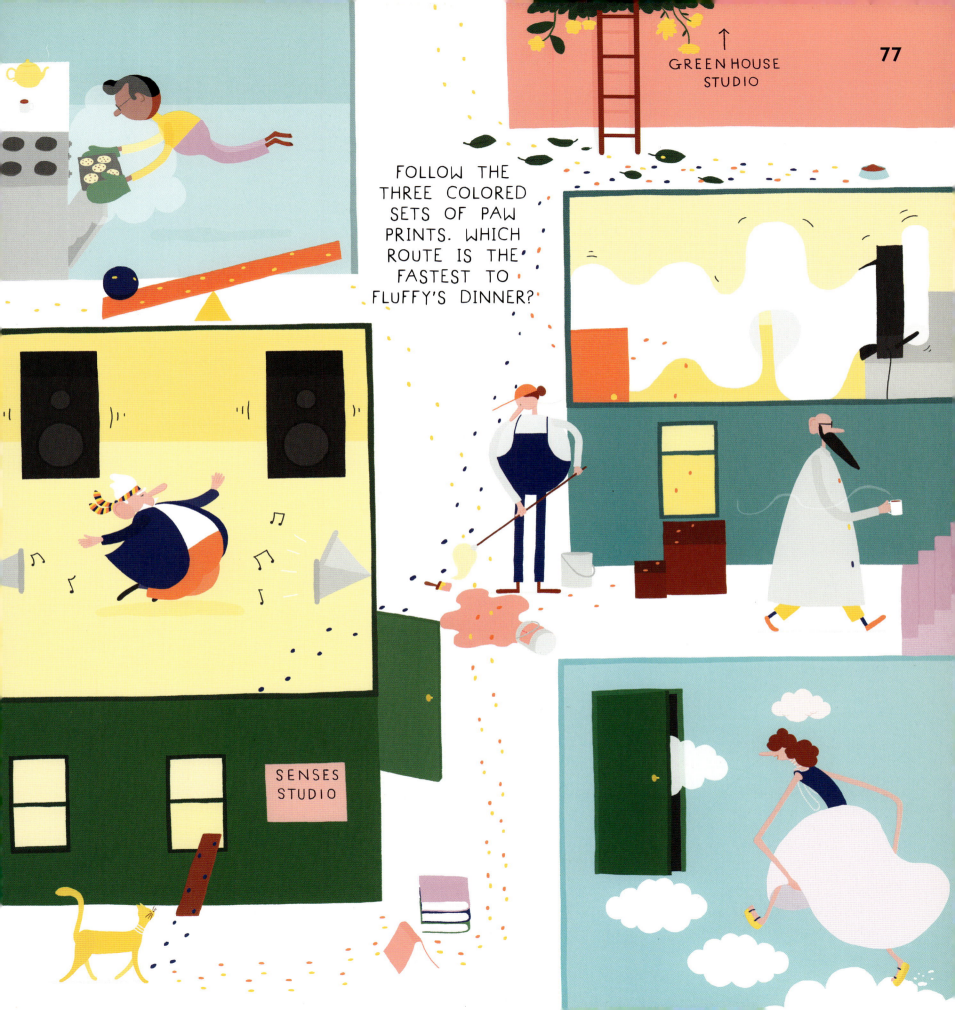

GREEN HOUSE
STUDIO

FOLLOW THE
THREE COLORED
SETS OF PAW
PRINTS. WHICH
ROUTE IS THE
FASTEST TO
FLUFFY'S DINNER?

SENSES
STUDIO

How can we tell a story by using pictures?

The Professor of Ideas knew there were other ways in which a visual could be used to communicate ideas.

"Who wants to pluck our first design challenge out of my cloud?" she asked.

The Professor of Making pulled out of the Professor of Ideas' cloud a small section of fluffiness that she then stretched and gave the shape of a comic book.

"A comic is a form of communication that helps us tell stories. For example, we can use one to convey information about the monarch butterflies that we have living here in the School of Art," said the professor.

The Professor of the Planet was delighted to hear this. He had been nurturing these exotic butterflies in his Greenhouse Studio, but recently he had heard some people in the community grumbling that the caterpillars had been eating the plants, and asking to have them removed. But without the caterpillars, the butterflies would disappear, too!

The Professor of Making continued. "Do you remember the lesson we had about the grid? Comics are divided on the page into a grid creating a series of frames. These frames create a sequence, becoming the windows through which you see action taking place. By putting into each frame a different image we can tell a story; one which has a beginning, a middle, and an end. And, in our case, our story will help inform the reader that if we want to protect the monarch butterflies in the school, we also have to protect the caterpillars!"

"But how do I use the images to tell the story?" asked the Professor of Form.

"In the same way you would write out a story. You need to consider who, when, and where; state the problem and what happened; and provide an ending. Draw one frame at a time, thinking about the actions of each of your characters within each frame," answered the Professor of Making.

The professors all nodded. They understood that comics could be a way of telling a story through pictures and words that would inform the community about protecting the precious caterpillars.

"I have an idea on how we should start the story!" said the Professor of the Planet, and so they began.

IN A COMIC, WE TELL A STORY BY SHOWING A DIFFERENT ACTION IN EVERY FRAME

ACTIVITY

Using a comic format, try telling a story to your friends. Think of the reasons why water is precious, and suggest ways in which they can help use less water. Make sure your comic has a beginning, a middle, and an end!

YOU ARE SAVING THE BUTTERFLY!

How can we recycle things to make art?

RECYCLING SHOWS US THAT THERE ARE ALL KINDS OF WAYS TO REUSE SOMETHING!

"Who wants to choose our next design challenge?" asked the Professor of Ideas.

This time the Professor of the Planet plucked out of the Professor of Ideas' cloud a small piece of fluffiness that he then expanded into the shape of a plastic bag.

The next challenge was to draw a diagram to show the ways in which plastic bags from the School of Art shop could be recycled.

"If you think about it, a plastic bag has a life cycle just like the monarch butterfly," said the Professor of the Planet. Everyone looked confused. "As we showed in the comic before, the monarch butterfly has four stages of its life cycle: egg, caterpillar, chrysalis, and butterfly."

The other professors nodded.

"Well, a plastic bag has a life cycle, even through it is a man-made product. It is made from plastic, used to carry things (often just once), thrown away, and sent to a landfill, where it takes up to 1,000 years to decompose! Now that you have an idea of where plastic bags come from and realize that it takes a long time for the material to physically break down, can you think of new ways of recycling the bags?"

The design challenge had been set!

The Professor of Making cut out one-inch strips of old plastic bags to use as a kind of yarn. Then she knit a new, fashionable bag for shopping out of the plastic strips.

The Professor of Form took his disused plastic bags and made a colorful chair for outdoors, making the most of the strength of the woven material.

The Professor of Senses wanted to travel to new heights and reinvigorate his senses. The Argentinian artist Tomás Saraceno, who designed a solar-powered hot-air balloon made out of hundreds of reused plastic bags, inspired him. Just like Saraceno he wanted to raise awareness of global climate change through the innovative reuse of plastic bags.

ONE MATERIAL TO RECYCLE...
LOTS OF IMAGINATIVE OPTIONS!

How can we show factual information using art?

The afternoon's next lesson took place in the Professor of Making's studio. The Professor of Ideas knew it was time for the others to learn more about different ways of collecting information and making sense of this through images. The world was changing and "data" was everywhere!

She knew that the Professor of Making would be able to help her explain how complex data could be made easier to understand through a process called "data visualization." Sometimes this process was also called "information graphics," or "infographics."

The Professor of Ideas explained, "Big data is really, really massive. It's lots and lots of numbers, which are captured and analyzed. Scientists and mathematicians work with big data in order to discover patterns in the information so that they can predict reliably what might happen in the future, like health trends, or how the climate could change over time."

"Small data is about personal information and can say something about ourselves," she continued.

"As artists, we can translate these numbers into images, visualizing the data to help make it easier to understand, with charts, diagrams, maps, pictograms, and even interactive artworks."

"I have been counting how many light bulbs have been left on or turned off at the end of each day in the School of Art," said the Professor of the Planet. "There are nearly three times more lights left on than switched off! How could we show this information and encourage people to improve energy efficiency at the School of Art? Just think, if everyone in the world turned off the lights when they were not in use, how much energy would be saved!" And so the professors set about finding the most imaginative way of showing this information, and came up with an idea...

ACTIVITY

Create your own infographic! Take some grid paper. On one side, fill a square for every piece of trash you throw away in one day. On the other side, fill a square for each item you recycle. Compare the two—which do you do more?

ON

OFF

AN INFOGRAPHIC SHOWING
THAT MORE LIGHT BULBS ARE
LEFT ON COMPARED TO THE LIGHT
BULBS THAT ARE SWITCHED OFF IN
THE SCHOOL OF ART AT NIGHT

How can we communicate with an audience when we are not there?

ACTIVITY

Design a different kind of announcement for the professors' meeting. Would you prefer to make a video, a 3-D object, or another kind of picture? What do you think would make people notice it best?

COMMUNICATIONS, SUCH AS POSTERS, ALLOW YOU TO GIVE INFORMATION TO SOMEONE WITHOUT BEING THERE YOURSELF

The next day the Professor of the Planet came to school with a question.

"How can we use what we have learned about saving energy and share it with others outside of the School of Art?" he asked.

"Yes, and how can we make them care about it?" said the Professor of Senses.

"Think about communication as if you were having a conversation with someone else. If you aren't there to speak to them yourself, you can send a set of words or pictures (such as a poster or a video) to them instead, and they then receive your message," replied the Professor of Ideas. "You need to have an idea of who your audience is and then think about the best way of communicating to them. How can you make that person care about what you have to say?"

"Okay," said the Professor of the Planet. "What if we helped our neighbors to understand that when they turn off their lights, it will help them save energy in their own homes—and help our planet!"

"Good idea!" said the Professor of Senses, adding, "We could also suggest they use energy-efficient lightbulbs!" Everyone smiled.

"I know!" said the Professor of Ideas. "Let's invite all our neighbors for a meeting. We could work together to save energy."

"We will also get to know our neighbors better!" added the Professor of the Planet.

Everyone thought this idea of involving other people in helping find solutions to a mutual problem was a good one.

"This process of working together to find a solution is called 'co-creation.' By having conversations with others where everyone has an equal say, people are encouraged to create solutions together."

"But how should we let them know about the meeting?" asked the Professor of Senses.

"Let's make a poster and put it on lampposts down the street!" said the Professor of Making. "That way, all our neighbors will see it."

What is "experimentation," and how does it help us to make art?

The professors knew that they only had two more lessons to go before they had to finish their works for the School of Art exhibition.

"Now it is time to take what we know and try to do something different with it that we haven't tried before. The next design challenge is to experiment!" said the Professor of Ideas. "Get your sketchbooks out! These are the perfect place for experimentation."

Through the year, the professors had kept sketchbooks, with notes about their ideas and where the ideas had come from, who inspired them, and new materials and techniques they had used. They had also written down the reflections they'd had as they were making their work.

The Professor of Making had used her digital tablet to create a virtual sketchbook, while the Professor of Senses pasted into his sketchbook examples of unusual sounds, smells, and textures. The Professor of Ideas kept her sketchbook in her cloud, the Professor of the Planet had a small, recycled sketchbook, and the Professor of Form carried around a large red box where his ideas were collected.

"A sketchbook is a place where you can take risks and challenge your normal ways of doing things. It is also a good place for thinking about how your work could have turned out if you had done things differently," said the Professor of Ideas. She then suggested that each professor randomly select from their sketchbook two ideas and put them side by side, and see if they could make a connection between the two. From this, a new and exciting idea might emerge.

By the end of the day, the professors' studios were filled with lots of new ideas from all the experimenting they had done.

BY TRYING THINGS YOU'VE NEVER DONE BEFORE, YOU CAN HAVE NEW IDEAS

ACTIVITY

Take an old magazine and cut out 20 words and 20 images. Put them in two separate envelopes, and, with your eyes closed, pull out one image and one word. Paste them in your sketchbook side by side. What ideas do they give you?

Lesson 40

What do we mean by "aesthetics"?

AESTHETICS ARE
JUDGEMENTS
WE MAKE ABOUT
HOW AN
ARTWORK LOOKS

ACTIVITY
Choose an artwork and describe what you see when you look at it. What basic elements do you see? Is the painting made up of lines, shapes, and color, and how do these change how you feel about it? What is your opinion about the work? Compare your answers with your friends'.

It was the last lesson before the exhibition and the professors were starting to think about how other people might respond to their work.

This lesson was about a very abstract concept called "aesthetics." This was to do with how we really "see" and appreciate our work and that of other artists and designers.

The Professor of Senses decided to try and explain aesthetics to his colleagues.

"Today," he announced, "you will ask questions of each other's work: is the work pleasing to the eye? Would you say that the work is beautiful—and also, what does it mean to be beautiful?"

He knew that there wasn't a correct answer and that what someone might think about a piece of art and design is a very personal reaction. He knew that every response would be different, because each of them had a different background, culture, and training, which might affect what they thought looked good or worked well.

But he also knew that if the professors had learned their lessons well and understood the basic elements of art and its principles, then this would provide them with a set of criteria that would help making an aesthetic judgement easier.

"To have an aesthetic experience means having a connection with a piece of art or design. Lines, textures, shapes, and colors are part of our vocabulary and these make us respond with our senses," explained the Professor of Senses. "When you look at the work you have done, what worked well and not so well in terms of the composition you created? Do the colors work well together and are the proportions of each shape pleasing to the eye? Does the work achieve what you meant it to, and what does it communicate to the viewer? Do you enjoy what you see?"

The last thing the Professor of Senses now asked was also one of the most important. "Have we had fun learning together?"

The professors decided that the lessons had sometimes been serious, but also playful and experimental. They had learned to become more curious and explore new ways of thinking about the world around them! The School of Art had taught all the professors that they could apply basic design principles to make beautiful things.

"We must get ready for our annual exhibition!" said the Professor of Ideas, interrupting the Professor of Senses' deep thoughts, and all the professors scurried back to their studios in preparation for the exhibition.

The Final Exhibition

The day of the Final Exhibition had finally arrived! The atmosphere was buzzing with excitement. Everyone had been busy finishing their work, the studios had been emptied, and the builders had made plinths and frames for each of the artworks.

The Professor of Ideas looked around the corner and spied a really long line of people as far as the eye could see. She smiled proudly.

"Please gather around," she called. All the professors stood together, and Fluffy the cat joined them. "The final exhibition plays an important role at the School of Art. An exhibition is where we all come together to show what we have made, and share it with a wider audience. Our exhibition is a place where you may look back on your success, and think about whether you have achieved what you set out to with a particular piece of art or design work. Be open to other people's feedback, as this is a chance to discuss how your work could be made better."

"Mostly it is a celebration of your achievements!" added the Professor of Senses, stepping up. "You have come a long way as students of the School of Art. You have learned about the basic design elements, how to experiment with different ideas and materials, how to use the basic principles, and, finally, how to use your new skills."

Agreeing with her friend, the Professor of Ideas had the final word.

"We hope that you will be inspired to make art and explore the world of design throughout your lives. It is a great way to make friends and to give so much back to the world. Thank you for your work this year in the School of Art!" And with that, she flung open the doors to the School of Art so that it was officially open to the public.

NAME _____
MEDIUM _____
YEAR _____

ADD YOUR OWN ARTWORK TO THE EXHIBITION

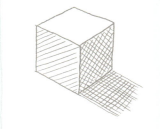

SCHOOL
OF ART
SHOW

Glossary

What do these words mean when we use them in art and design?

A

ABSTRACT – An idea or thought without a physical form.

AESTHETIC – Relating to the beauty of a particular object.

ALIGNMENT – An arrangement or positioning based on straight lines.

ANALOGOUS – Describes colors found next to each other on a color wheel.

APPEARANCE – The way that something looks.

ARRANGEMENT – The manner in which things have been ordered or positioned.

ARTIST – The creator of an original piece of creative work.

ASYMMETRY – Designed with unequal sides or halves along an axis.

AUDIENCE – People who look at, or experience, a design or artwork.

B

BACKGROUND – The part of a scene farthest from the viewer.

BALANCE – Even distribution of weight.

BASIC ELEMENT – A building block of art and design.

C

CANVAS – Stretched material, ready to be painted on.

CERAMIC – A form of pottery, made of clay and hardened by firing.

COLLAGE – Technique of composing various pieces of paper, objects, and other materials together.

COMIC – A visual story told in a series of frames.

COMMUNICATION – An exchange between two or more people (a sender and a receiver).

COMPLEMENTARY – Something that enhances a certain quality (e.g., brightness) of an object.

COMPOSITION – The deliberate arrangement of elements.

CONCEPT – Idea or thought.

CONTRAST – A relational difference.

CROSSHATCH MARKS (also: crosshatching) – A kind of shading made from intersecting parallel lines.

CUBE – A three-dimensional object, based on a square, with six equal surfaces.

D

DESIGNER – A person who plans, organizes, and decides what something looks like and how it functions

DIRECTION – Showing visual movement pointing toward something.

DRAWING – A picture or sketch usually made with lines.

E

ELEMENT (see: basic element)

ENVIRONMENT – An object's surroundings.

EXHIBITION – A single or group of artworks presented to an audience.

EXPERIMENTATION – To try something different, but in an orderly way; to test something.

F

FLAT – Without depth, or volume.

FOREGROUND – The part of a scene closest to the viewer.

FORM – Something's shape or visible structure.

FORMAL STRUCTURE – A composition based on order.

FRAME – The edge or boundaries of an image; a structure that surrounds an artwork.

G

GEOMETRIC – Based on relational lines, shapes, and forms.

GRID – A series of modular units, equally spaced with intersecting lines, which helps an artist or designer to organize the elements in a composition.

H

HARMONY – A pleasing effect, often created by combining elements that share similar properties (e.g., colors).

HIERARCHY – An ordering or arrangement that causes you to notice certain elements before others.

HORIZON – A line in the distance where the sky meets the ground.

HORIZONTAL – A line that runs from side to side, parallel to the horizon.

HUE – A pure color.

I

ILLUSION – A trick of the eye.

ILLUSTRATION – A picture or image.

INFOGRAPHIC – A visual representation that conveys complex information.

INFORMAL STRUCTURE – A composition based on disorder.

INTERACTION – The reaction between two elements when they are seen together.

L

LINE – A singular, straight length comprised of a series of points.

M

MOTIF – A decorative design.

MOVEMENT – An illusion or perception of direction across a composition.

N

NEGATIVE SPACE – The background space around a drawing.

O

ORDER – The formal arrangement of elements.

P

PATTERN – The effect of the same element repeated regularly multiple times.

PERSPECTIVE – The effect that causes things to appear smaller in the background.

PHOTOGRAPH (also: photo) – An image created by light using a camera or similar device.

PORTRAIT – A representation or likeness of a person.

POSITIVE SPACE – The "filled-in" area of a composition.

PRIMARY COLOR – A color that cannot be made by mixing other colors.

PROFILE – A person's face, seen from the side.

PROPORTION – The size of one part in relation to the whole.

R

REALISTIC – Lifelike.

RECYCLE – To reuse waste for a new purpose.

REPETITION – The same element reappearing in a regular pattern.

RHYTHM – Movement repeated over time.

S

SCALE – The relationship between the size of two objects.

SCULPTURE – A three-dimensional visual form.

SECONDARY COLOR – A color made by mixing two primary colors together.

SHADE – A color where black has been added.

SHADING – Mark-making that gives an image tone, suggesting light and shade.

SHAPE – A two-dimensional form, without depth.

SILHOUETTE – A picture of a person's profile in outline, often colored in black.

SKETCH – A quick or preparatory drawing.

SKETCHBOOK – A book in which to make sketches and notes, and collect ideas.

STUDIO – A room in which to create.

SURFACE – An object's outer shell.

SYMMETRY – Where an image is reflected down its central axis.

T

TANGIBLE – Something that can be touched or held.

TERTIARY COLOR – A color made by mixing a primary color with a secondary color.

TEXTURE – The feel of an object's surface.

TWO-DIMENSIONAL – Flat; with height and width, but without volume.

TINT – A color where white has been added.

TONE – A color where gray has been added.

THREE-DIMENSIONAL – With volume: height, width, and depth.

V

VERTICAL – A line that runs from top to bottom, at right angles to the horizon.

VIEWER – The person looking at an artwork or design.

VIRTUAL – That which is not tangible; an object that cannot be held; often used to describe something that you encounter digitally or with a computer.

A VISUAL – Something, such as a map, used to describe or display thoughts, ideas, or information.

VOLUME – The three-dimensional space contained inside an object.

W

WEIGHT – The heaviness or lightness of something.

Bibliography — Who has inspired us at the School of Art?

JOSEF ALBERS (1963)
Interaction of Color
New Haven: Yale University Press

RUDOLF ARNHEIM (1954)
Art and Visual Perception
Berkeley: University of California Press

KEN BAYNES (1976)
About Design
London: Design Council Publications

DONIS A. DONDIS (1974)
A Visual Primer of Visual Literacy
Cambridge: The MIT Press

KARL GERSTNER (2001)
Visual Language
New York: Hatje Cantz Publishers

PETER GREEN (1974)
*Design Education: Problem
Solving and Visual Experience*
London: BT Batsford Ltd

ARMIN HOFMANN and
GEORGE NELSON (1965)
*Graphic Design Manual:
Principles and Practice*
New York: Van Nostrand Reinhold

JOHANNES ITTEN (1961)
*The Art of Color: The Subjective Experience
and Objective Rationale of Color*
New York: Reinhold
Publishing Corporation

GYORGY KEPES (1965) (ed.)
Education of Vision
New York: George Braziller

PAUL KLEE (1944)
Pedagogical Sketchbook
New York: Nierendorf Gallery

CHRISTIAN LEBORG (2006)
Visual Grammar
New York: Princeton Architectural Press

ELLEN LUPTON and
JENNIFER COLE PHILLIPS (2008)
Graphic Design: The New Basics
New York: Princeton Architectural Press

DORTHEA C. MALCOLM (1972)
Design: Elements and Principles
Worcester, Massachusetts: Davis
Publications Inc.

W. H. MAYHALL (1979)
Principles in Design
London: Design Council

LAZLO MOHOLY-NAGY (1946)
Vision in Motion
Chicago: Paul Theobald and Co.

JOSEF MÜLLER-BROCKMANN (1996)
Grid Systems in Graphic Design
Santa Monica: Ram Publications

GEORGE NELSON (1979)
*How to See: A Guide to Reading
Our Man-Made Environment*
New York: Little, Brown and Company

MAURICE DE SAUSMAREZ (1964)
Basic Design: The Dynamics of Visual Form
Worthing, West Sussex: Littlehampton
Book Services Ltd

ALEX W. WHITE (2011)
The Elements of Graphic Design
New York: Allworth Press

WUCIUS WONG (1993)
Principles of Form and Design
New York: John Wiley & Sons, Inc.

THIS BOOK IS DEDICATED TO ART
AND DESIGN STUDENTS EVERYWHERE.

Wide Eyed Editions
www.wideeyededitions.com

The School of Art copyright © Aurum Press Ltd 2015
Illustrations copyright © Daniel Frost 2015
Text copyright © Teal Triggs 2015

First published in the United States in 2015 by Wide Eyed Editions
an imprint of Quarto Inc.,
276 Fifth Avenue, Suite 206, New York, NY 10001.
www.wideeyededitions.com

ISBN 978-1-84780-700-7

The illustrations were created digitally
Set in Gill Sans and School of Art

Designed by Joe Hales
Edited by Jenny Broom
Published by Rachel Williams

Printed in Dongguan, Guangdong, China

1 3 5 7 9 8 6 4 2